Lessons Learned as a Bridesmaid

what every single woman should know
before becoming a bride

Larissa Dayana Jean

WESTBOW
PRESS
A DIVISION OF THOMAS NELSON

Cover image and design by Lindsey Meyer, Meyer Inspired Photography
www.meyerinspired.com

WestBow Press books may be ordered through booksellers or by contacting:

WestBow Press
A Division of Thomas Nelson
1663 Liberty Drive
Bloomington, IN 47403
www.westbowpress.com
1-(866) 928-1240

ISBN: 978-1-4497-1814-5 (sc)
ISBN: 978-1-4497-1813-8 (e)
ISBN: 978-1-4497-1815-2 (hc)
Library of Congress Control Number: 2011930114
Printed in the United States of America
WestBow Press rev. date: 6/29/2011

This book is dedicated to all bridesmaids who are waiting to be a bride. Be encouraged; God's timing is perfect.

"Wait on the Lord; be of good courage, and He shall strengthen your heart; Wait, I say, on the Lord!"
(Ps 27:14)

Contents

Acknowledgments

FATHER GOD, I FIRST WANT TO thank you for your love, your good plan for my life, and the honor of sharing what you have deposited in me with others. Thank you for the wait, the heartaches, and even the disappointments. Even these have worked out for my good, and have brought me one step closer to my divine purpose. I love you with all of my heart, mind, and soul.

To my immediate family: *Mommie* and *Papi,* thank you both for being wonderful parents to me and training me up in the way I should go. I could never stop saying *thank you* for all of the wisdom, love, guidance, and protection you have imparted in my life. I love you both with all my heart. *Grama, je t'aime.* You are truly one of the women of God who has influenced my life the most. Thank you for your love, care, wisdom, hugs, good food, and listening ear throughout my life. *Richie* and *Cliff,* I *love* being your older sister! You two make me so very proud. Thank you for listening to my ideas, inspiring me, and supporting me while writing this book. I love you both so very much.

To all of my extended family in Massachusetts, New York, New Jersey, Connecticut, Florida, Georgia, Canada, France, and Haiti: I love you all so much. Thank you for being a blessing to me each in your own special way.

To the Good Samaritan Church: Thank you for being my first church family and laying the foundation for my walk with the Lord. I thank you all for nurturing me, teaching me, and caring for me. I love you all.

To Pastor Brave and Ma Pas: Thank you for being my first set of parents in the Lord. You have always treated me like your own daughter, and for that, I do thank you. Thank you for your love, encouragement, and prayers throughout the years! I love you both!

To Eunone: I love you from the bottom of my heart. You are the big sister that I've always wanted. Thank you for our Wolf Pack (inside joke), and taking me under your wings when I first moved to Georgia. Thank you for your love, words of wisdom, advice and listening ear during my teen years and now adult years. You have been more of a blessing to me than you'll ever know.

To Eunos: Growing up, you were the older brother that I always wanted. Thank you for treating me like your little sister. I love you so much. You have always been an amazing example to me. I have learned so much from the life you lead.

To the Etienne family: By far, the dearest family to me. I consider you all my lifelong friends. Thank you for your sincerity, your love and adoration for the Father. Your family and ministry inspire me so much. Your support and enthusiasm during this project has been such an encouragement to me. I love you all more than you know!

To Pastor Vercane and Mommie Vercane: I love you both very much. Thank you for being such a blessing to me and to my family for so many years. Thank you for loving me as your second daughter.

To Pastor Mardochee, Brother Ronix, Brother Formose, and Brother Watson: As a young girl growing up in the house of God, you four were truly the pillars of the youth. Thank you for being such godly examples of true men of God and all the things I desire in a husband one day. I love you all *so* much! Thank you for planting good seeds in my life; my life is evidence of the fruit of your labor.

To my Joshua Generation Campus Ministry leaders, Elder Gregg, Sister Carol, Ayana, Reggie, Tracy, and Rob: I love you guys! Wow, how different would my college years have been without your love and support? Thank you for truly nurturing me and helping me grow as a young adult during my time at UGA.

To Omega Worship Center: I love you, Omega family! I probably would not have enough space to fit it all on one page, but from the bottom of my heart, I love each and every one of you. I love this ministry. Thank you for your love, support, encouragement while writing this book, and your unquenchable love for God! I couldn't imagine not having each of you in my life.

To my mother in Christ and Pastor, Dr. Yulonda Z. Lewis: You are my Naomi. I love you from the *bottom* of my heart. Thank you for mothering me, teaching me, encouraging me, praying with *and* for me. Thank you also for the beautiful foreword. You are amazing! I admire you and aspire to be like you in so many ways. Thank you, thank you, THANK YOU.

To my father in Christ and Pastor, Bishop Rayfield Lewis: I thank God for you *every* day. Thank you for being such a blessing to me, loving me, and for being an awesome father in the Lord to me. Thank you for your hugs! Thank you for being a part of my editing team! You have taught me so much just by the life you live daily. I respect you, admire you, honor you, and *love* you dearly. You will always have a special place in my heart.

To the prayer warriors: Pastor Smith, I love you with all of my heart. Thank you for your compassion, understanding, and support. Thank you for always encouraging me to press on, especially with this book. Thank you for encouraging me to "write the vision and make it plain", as pertains to this book down. I am so grateful to have you in my life. *Elder Cal,* thank you for your words of life and teaching me how to be a prayer warrior. I love you so much!

Minister Anderson, thank you for loving me, believing in me, and constantly lifting me up in prayer. I love you dearly.

Sister Natasha, I love you, Tasha! Wow, if I was to look up *encouragement* in the dictionary, your name and picture would be there! Thank you for *believing* in me and the vision that God gave me with this book. Your little texts that said, "How's the book coming along?" meant more to me than you'll ever know. Thank you for being my sister.

June, I'm *so* grateful that God would allow us to cross paths that day at the SLC bathroom! I love you *more* than you'll know. Thank you for pushing me to be better, encouraging me, praying for me, and being an older sister to me. You mean so much to me.

Deaconess Booker: I love you *so* dearly. Thank you for the countless times I would call you and you would be there to help me through whatever the situation. I appreciate you *so* much. I value our friendship and the relationship that we have. You are truly one of the many women of God that I admire the most in my life. Thank you for always opening your home to me. Your words of wisdom have encouraged me during my waiting season. Thank you for always cheering me on. Hugs!

To Elder Talibah Durham: I love you. You were so influential in my young adult years, and for that, I thank you. Thank you for also pushing me to grow, molding me to be a leader, especially in campus ministry. Thank you for helping make my years in college so full of great memories.

To Chanell: ¡*Querida, te amo muchísimo!* I love you, Chanell! Thank you for always being so encouraging and supportive, especially throughout the process of writing this book. You have always been a shoulder to lean on and an ear to listen. You are *such* a jewel in the earth and a precious gift from God. I value your friendship *so* much. Thank God for *you*.

To Tiffany S. King: Teacakes! Girl, you know how much I love you! Thank you so much for being one of my editors for the book. Your input as one of my editors, and advice during the publishing process meant the *world* to me. Thank you for always being real with me and "telling me like it is"! Thank you for *always* being there when I needed you. But most importantly, thank you for loving me, and being a true friend. You mean so much to me, and I am so grateful to the Lord for blessing me with an awesome sister like you. You are the best!

To Chris: Cristobal, thank you for being such a real friend. We have so many years of an awesome friendship. I appreciate you so much! Thank you for being my marketing guru. You're awesome! Thank you for also believing in the vision for this book, and always having my back through thick and thin. I love you, man!

To Lindsey Meyer (www.meyerinspired.com): Thank you *so* much for the beautiful pictures, your patience during *all* the editing, and designing my front and cover! You are such a blessing to me!

To Antwon Davis (www.AntwonDavis.com): Antwon, you did such an *awesome* job with my website! Thank you so much and may the Lord richly bless your gift of creativity.

To the staff at Westbow Press: Thank you for partnering with me and turning my dream of being a published author into a reality.

To dear friends near and far: Thank you for your encouragement during this journey to being a published author. I thank you and love you all!

And finally, to the most inspiring godly marriages in my life: Levy and Eunone Dorcely, Eunos and Jetsie Laverdure, Edmond and Eunice Coley, Travis and Triana Walker, Tobin and Joanne Shoemate, Eric and Frankie Gilmore, Gary and Carissa Messado, Formose and Travice

Obas, Fred and Sterlande Altidor, Ronix and Gerda St. Germain, Watson and Carol Escarment, Pastor Mardochee and Roslie Pardieu, Antonio and Valerie Blue, Elder Gregg and Carol Johnson, Reggie and Ayana Mackey, Rob and Tracy Mathis, Christopher and Chastity Eggleston, Keith and Cristy Campbell, Victor and Betty Booker, and Bishop Rayfield and Dr. Yulonda Lewis. Thank you *all* for being such wonderful examples of godly marriages. Your marriages inspire me and encourage me to keep believing that it *is* possible to marry the man or woman of your dreams. I love you all!

Words from the Heart

by Dr. Yulonda Z. Lewis

LARISSA DAYANA JEAN, SOMEONE ONCE DEFINED intimacy as "into-me-I-see". It was absolutely not about what was seen in you as a bridesmaid, but more about enhancing the bride's day.

In the college town of Athens, Georgia, home of the University of Georgia, I have had the great pleasure and honor to serve as her pastor and mentor, and to the many students who find themselves caught between an earthly launching pad, the university, and a Godly landing place, at a church known as Omega Worship Center.

The common theme with the students I pastor is assisting them in transitioning from young adulthood to babes in Christ, and from family expectations to God's ultimate call. As a result, when I met Larissa, as a humble and soft-spoken young lady in the midst of other tenacious and out-spoken college students, I wasn't surprised that her transitional testimony would cause her to make some tough decisions; much like the experience of other students I had previously encountered.

However, what stood out to me about Larissa was that her humility in God became her strength to go in whatever direction God led her, in spite of the obstacles she faced. Since God guided her to Omega Worship

Center, at a point in her life where His divine leading became greater than even her cultural ties, I was only led to nurture and confirm what God was doing in her, as she undoubtedly postured herself to embrace the unchartered path He was leading her down. As I watched her continue to grow in God, I noticed that the timeline of major events and plans that were expected for her life (whether these expectations were from family, friends or even from Larissa herself), were purposefully being broken. It was as if God had been divinely revealing a new and special timeline. I was watching Him replace man's timeline for her with His own Lifeline. This lifeline would definitely involve God's plan for her as it relates to marriage. It included a journey which surprisingly involved a lot of dresses that would indeed lead to a lot of lessons. Certainly, God works in mysterious ways!

Being once engaged and a bridesmaid far too many times than any single lady would dream of (especially since young women almost all dream only of being the bride) God walks Larissa down the aisle to marry a piece of her divine destiny, which is this literary work, *Lessons Learned as a Bridesmaid*. I truly thank God for the path that He has laid for her no matter how strange it may seem to man. His plan is definitely full of purpose, which is a purpose that so many other single women may glean from before they walk down the aisle and say "I do." Thus, I call all single ladies to position themselves to read this book and to catch every lesson that is shared as if they were catching a bride's beautiful bouquet; because much like the bouquet, you can expect *Lessons Learned as a Bridesmaid* to positively bless the next bride to be!

Dr. Yulonda Z. Lewis
Senior Pastor
Omega Worship Center
Athens, Georgia

Introduction

THE DRESS FIT LIKE A DREAM; my hair was just the way I wanted it, and there were only five minutes to go until it was time to walk down the aisle—only it wasn't *my* special day. I was just the bridesmaid. Today (as many other times before) it was my friend's day to shine. It was my turn to wait.

I have attended *twenty-four* weddings! Being a bridesmaid has almost become like a hobby for me, an annual summer pastime, as many of my closest friends will say jokingly. I have been a flower girl twice, a wedding soloist once, and a bridesmaid *seven* times! If you were to compare me to Katherine Heigl's character from the romantic comedy, *27 Dresses,* we would come neck-and-neck; I would just be the black-girl version. Now, this is not in the *least* my way of venting my frustrations of being in so many weddings; nor is this the old-time gripe, "Always a bridesmaid, never a bride." Truth be told, I really do enjoy going to and being a part of weddings. The God-instituted establishment of holy matrimony, with the exchange of vows, flower girls, and yes, those (at times) unflattering bridesmaid's dresses, makes this special event very memorable.

However, this is not what my story is about. This book is dedicated to all the ladies who may not feel as overjoyed to hear of yet another friend's recent engagement. This is for the young ladies who, as happy as they may feel to see a friend marry the person of their dreams, have that little ache in their hearts that says, "God, when will it be *my* turn?" My story is all about how to wait with contentment for your husband that God has chosen just for *you*.

I pour out my heart to you in this book. My prayer is that something will be said that will encourage your heart and remind you that 1) God has *not* forgotten about you; 2) It's really not *our* job to figure out when we will finally be married; and 3) To remember this Scripture when the wait gets hard: "Wait on the Lord. Be of good courage and He will strengthen your heart. Wait, I say, on the Lord."[1] So what does it mean to *wait?* It means to **W**illingly **A**ccept **I**mmanuel's **T**iming. Let us wait with expectation on Him who rewards those who diligently seek Him.

Love,
Larissa D. Jean

---

1   Psalm 27:14 NKJV.

1

The Candy Apple Dress

"THE NEXT WEDDING YOU WALK IN, it *better* be your own!" my dad said in exasperation as he dished out more money to pay for expenses of another person's wedding. Now, had I been in his shoes, I would have probably told my daughter the same thing. If you have ever been a bridesmaid (and if you haven't, you probably will … unless, of course, you're male), you and I both know the saga it entails to aid in making another person's wedding day just right. First, after receiving the invitation to be a bridesmaid, you must then agree to do so; this is key! Secondly, in "Being a Bridesmaid 101," you have to count the cost—*literally*. Even Jesus told his disciples to count the cost to follow him. You must take into consideration the cost of: the dress (which is yours to have and to mold), the shoes, the accessories, the hairdo, the nails, the makeup, the bridal shower, and the wedding gift. Now, being Haitian-American, and attending as many Haitian weddings as I have (most of which can be very extravagant), these costs add up. So you can see now why my dad was just a bit annoyed at the idea of helping me pay for another friend's wedding.

However, this particular bridesmaid experience in the summer of 2006 was different. Up until now, I can honestly say that out of all of my dresses, this one was my favorite. A sister at my church at the time asked me to walk in her wedding. It was the summer before my fourth year in college. The dress was absolutely beautiful—candy apple red. It was the first bridesmaid dress that I really liked and could wear again. Not only did I walk in that particular wedding that year, but I was a bridesmaid in another friend's wedding and attended one more that summer. Now, to this day, I don't know if there was something in the water, but it seemed that *everyone* was getting bitten by the love bug, and the only vaccination to cure it was to get hitched. I am Haitian American, and that plays a huge role in this particular chapter of my life. Every young Haitian woman knows that by the age of eighteen, you *will* be bombarded by one family member after the next, *"Ou gen yon ti ménage?"* (In Haitian Creole, that means, "Do you have a boyfriend?") And of course, if you were anything like me growing up, having a "ménage" was pretty much out of the question ... until I finished with college. With my fourth year of college knocking on my door, it became the million-dollar question.

It seemed as if all of my friends either found their mate in college, while pursuing the coveted MRS. degree, or in church. Walking in so many people's weddings at church, I always envisioned that I would meet that oh-so-special someone at the house of God. It was almost like Jewish women in the Bible—all the good Jewish girls always seemed to meet a nice Jewish boy at the well. Hey, it worked for Rachel and Rebekah. Perhaps it would be my turn soon.

Fall 2006, much to my surprise, was the very first time I would fall in love. At the age of twenty-one, I was finally in my first serious relationship. To say the least, it was the happiest I had been at that point in my life. It seemed like the picture-perfect match made in heaven. We attended the same church, even led the same campus ministry together. We were saved, filled with the Holy Ghost, and loved God—what could go wrong? As the relationship progressed, we talked about marriage, and we seriously considered making plans to have our own wedding bells ring—or so I thought. You see, if there was anything I learned through this experience, it was that God's ways are truly higher than our ways. During the waiting process, it's important to have an expectant hope that the manifestation of what God has promised will indeed come to pass in His perfect timing. We have to surrender our own timetable for God's and trust that His timing and His will is perfect for our lives.

My dreams of marrying the first boy I ever loved were brought to a screeching halt. The few days leading to the end of the relationship hit me from the blindside. I did not see it coming at the time, however in retrospect, I realized that were several warning signs. I noticed that he had been acting very strange. He was very withdrawn, quiet and seemed very on edge lately. The day before finals, after we had attended a ministry meeting, I decided to get some answers myself. I really did not understand what was going on with him, the relationship, or anything between us lately, so in the parking lot of my college apartment, I finally decided to get some answers from him.

"So, what is going on between us?" I asked, nervous about what I would hear. The next few words put my mind into a talespin: "I am pulling out of the relationship..." I was shocked. I was hurt. I was angry. I was confused. I was heartbroken. After a seven month relationship that went from zero to one hundred overnight, it was really over. Tearfully, I walked back into my apartment.

The first week following the end of the relationship was the most difficult time that I had to deal with up until that point in my life. I couldn't study for finals; I couldn't eat, and forget about sleeping well. All that I kept telling God was, "God, my heart hurts so badly right now. Will this hurt ever go away?" My heart was broken into a million pieces. Words cannot express how I felt when I realized the magnitude of the phrase, "It's over. I'm pulling out of the relationship." Feelings of rejection, alienation, and just not feeling "good enough" plagued my mind for weeks following the breakup. It didn't make the situation any better when I learned just a few months later that the young man really just wanted to pursue a mutual friend; another major blow.

Did it take a long time to get over? Absolutely! Can God heal a broken heart that seems beyond repair? Most certainly. The hardest thing that I have come to realize when it comes to waiting on God's timing is how incredibly *impatient* we are as His children. At times, our prayer may sound something like this: "Father, I trust you … just as long as you get me what I want before I'm twenty-five." How many times have we groaned and complained that God is taking just a bit longer that we would like?

At that season of my life, as much as I thought I was ready for marriage, and as much as I longed to be the bride just for once, it would not have changed God's sovereign plan. He is in total control. Until we connect to the Father's heart and know without a doubt that He is sovereign and has His overall plan and our good at the top of His list, it will be very difficult to wait gracefully on Immanuel's timing.

The summer of 2007 was the most difficult season of my life. Not only was I trying to wrap my mind around why God had allowed this painful breakup to occur, but now I had to face the embarrassment and pain of resending out the updated memo, which read: "To whom it may concern: Larissa will NOT be getting married to the guy after all. You can all go back to your lives now. Thanks." Was it God's fault that the relationship went sour? No. Was I too anxious, perhaps too eager to be a bride? Yes. You see, at that point in my life, I felt that marriage would help validate me before my family and friends. That is certainly not the right motive going into a marriage. A woman of God should seek her validation from God alone. He affirms your worth because He saw that you were worth dying for; that makes you pretty valuable all by itself!

The Word of God makes it crystal clear that we are not to be anxious for anything. I don't believe that God is fazed one bit by our lack of patience. He promises that in due time (meaning when He is *good and ready*) we will reap a harvest if we faint not. So hold on. Wait for God's timing—it's perfect. My worst year emotionally, 2007, was also the year of immense growth in the Lord. I believe that God has a way to cause us to draw closer into Him when it hurts the most. That summer, I learned to fall in love with Jesus all over again. As promised, He was very near to me in my state of broken-heartedness. I learned that God truly loved me with an unconditional, "no strings attached" kind of love. I had to learn the hard way that as exhilarating, new, and exciting a relationship with someone can be, no human can promise that they will be the same yesterday, today, and tomorrow. I learned to make Jesus my *first* love again.

That summer, I learned that even those who love God are not perfect, and as a result, they are prone to hurt you. However, we are all being perfected into the image of Christ. The Lord had to show me that I had put this young man on a pedestal. This is a dangerous thing to do, because the people we love the most will inevitably hurt us in one way or another. It was a humbling experience. After three years with a broken heart and carrying this hurt for so long, I finally asked the Lord to help me release the pain to Him and asked Him to heal me and to help me extend forgiveness. God is faithful to heal the hurt and restore your heart and make you whole again.

Notes from

The Candy Apple Dress

Confessions of a Bridesmaid

1. Describe your first serious relationship. How old were you? How did it make you feel?

2. How did this relationship affect your relationship with God and others?

Confessions of a Bridesmaid

3. Describe your first experience with heartache from a relationship that ended. How did you cope with it?

4. How did that relationship make you a better person?

2
Sarah's Waiting Process

THERE ARE TWO WOMEN IN THE Bible who I believe truly exemplify how to wait on the manifestation of God's promises and how *not* to do it: Hannah and Sarah. Let's look at my girl Sarah first.

"Now Sarai, Abram's wife, had borne him no children. And she had an Egyptian maidservant whose name was Hagar. So Sarai said to Abram, 'See now, the Lord has restrained me from bearing children. Please, go in to my maid; perhaps I shall obtain children by her.' And Abram heeded the voice of Sarai.'"[2] Although many sermons have been preached about Sarah and her anxiousness to bear children, my heart really goes out to Sarah in just this one verse. How does this relate to waiting on God's timing? Follow me here; I'm going somewhere.

My studies of Jewish biblical culture showed me that the desire for bearing children for a Jewish woman was intense. A barren woman was a disgrace for her husband, and it was legitimate grounds for him to divorce her. As a young girl, I would often liken this same intensity for

---

2   Genesis 16:1–2, NKJV.

young women in my community to find somebody and get married. It almost scared me when I hit eighteen, because it felt like there was this imaginary "expiration date" hidden somewhere on a Haitian girl. The label went something like this: "WARNING: MUST BE MARRIED *AT LEAST* BY TWENTY-ONE. AT TWENTY-FOUR, *YOU'RE PUSHING IT.* PLEASE DISPOSE OF AFTER TWENTY-FIVE IF *STILL* NOT MARRIED!"

As I was growing up in church, the quest to find a husband and get married was a message preached both subconsciously and quite blatantly at times, toward all the young ladies by older women. The acceptable timetable for most young ladies was to meet someone at eighteen, date the guy for about five to six years, and by twenty-three or twenty-four, you need to be married. So you can just imagine when I hit eighteen and I still had not met anyone, my initial thoughts were, *Yikes! I must be behind schedule—I need to be married in like the next four years!*

I really like to put myself in the shoes of the matriarchs and patriarchs of the faith. Can you imagine the overwhelming pressure Sarah experienced in waiting for the manifestation of God's promise to her and her husband, Abraham? I'm sure that there were many times in Sarah's heart when she would feel disheartened, seeing other friends who were being blessed with children while she was still waiting. If people threw baby showers during that time, Sarah probably thought at one time or another, "If I have to go to *another* baby shower, I'm gonna hurt somebody!" Ladies, you know how we can be sometimes!

The important lesson I believe the Lord needs us to really get during our season of expectant waiting is to trust first that His timing is *perfect.* I cannot stress that enough. But also, just as importantly, God has not forgotten about you. I don't care if it seems like you have been waiting for years and it *feels* like God has you up on a shelf, alone and forgotten. I encourage you to dismiss this lie of the enemy. We serve a loving Father, who hears every unspoken prayer, bottles every tear, and takes great pleasure in opening His hand to satisfy the desire of every living thing. Sarah's words truly caught my attention when she believed that the Lord had "restrained" her from having children, almost as if He had purposely withheld children from her to spite her. This, as we all know, could not have been further from the truth. God promises us that there is no good thing that He would withhold from us. Therefore, if it is your desire to be a wife and a mother one day, these are definitely good things in the eyes of the Father. And He can bless us with these things, in His timing.

I heard a message that Joyce Meyer preached that really blessed me in reference to waiting. She said that God is more concerned about how we endure the waiting period in our lives, more so than the manifestation of His promise to us coming to pass. God had already promised Abraham that he would be the father of many nations—the real test was how well Sarah could demonstrate her ability to wait on God's perfect timing for this great promise. We all know how the story goes—they didn't do very well. Sarah got anxious and decided to "help God out" by moving the plans along a little faster. So she convinced her husband to sleep with her maidservant, Hagar, thinking that by taking matters into her own hands, she could fix the whole "timing" situation. Perhaps you are reading this and you have never been married before. Let me encourage you today—be anxious for *nothing!* My dear sister, believe that God's promises are true when He says that there is a time for everything. Maybe you tried to "help God out" as it relates to relationships and you find yourself in a relationship that you know in your spirit is not of God. Maybe you have allowed the pressures of family and friends to push you into a relationship that is out of God's timing.

Look at Sarah as an example. Although she may have gotten what she *thought* she wanted, it cost her great emotional distress and drama that the Lord never intended for her to endure. That is what happens when we get anxious—we bring upon ourselves unnecessary turmoil into our lives. Despite Sarah's manipulation to get a child, she and Abraham *still* had to wait for the manifestation of God's promise, which was Isaac. Ladies, don't miss the husband that God has already chosen for you all along because of your flesh or pressure from other people. Because, like Sarah, you will go through all the pain and suffering settling for a counterfeit blessing, when all along, God had His blessing waiting for you. If God has promised you a husband, rest assured that in God's timing (again, when He is good and ready) He will bring it to pass. Don't get anxious. Wait on the promise!

Notes from
Sarah's Waiting Process

Confessions of a Bridesmaid

1. Describe a time in your life when it was hard to wait on God's timing.

2. When you were growing up, did you experience pressure from family and/or friends about getting married at a specific age?

3. List three things that you are waiting for God to do in your life while you are still single.

4. Have you ever found yourself in a relationship that was out of God's timing? What were the consequences?

3

Hannah's Waiting Process

WE HAVE LOOKED AT SARAH AND how she did not pass the waiting test very well. Now let's look at a woman who—although she had to wait longer than her flesh probably wanted to—still waited with such grace. I am talking about Hannah.

"Now there was a certain man of Ramathaim Zophim, of the mountains of Ephraim, and his name was Elkanah ... he had two wives: the name of one was Hannah, and the name of the other Penninah. Penninah had children, but Hannah had no children."[3] Again we see this "no children" dilemma.

Meanwhile, back on the ranch, I was knocking on nineteen years of age and *still* no prospects in sight! I mean *nowhere*! I can remember that year; I had just rededicated my life to the Lord at a United Campus Ministries conference in Atlanta, Georgia. Because I was so fired up and committed to living a life unto Lord, Satan of course, had to send a little counterfeit along the way to distract me from what God was doing in

_____
3   1 Samuel 1:1–2, NKJV.

my heart during my first year of college. It was a time to test how much of my heart I had really entrusted to the Lord as it related to this area of my life. Sadly, I realized that I still had not given every part of my heart over to God, including the area of the right relationships in His timing. So I took the bait.

It happened as one of those friend "hook up" things. A friend of mine at my church at the time had an older cousin who had expressed his interest in me. He was twenty-four, and I was nineteen. Besides feeling overly excited that I had caught the attention of an older guy, but I was thinking to myself as well, *Yes! I've finally made it to first base—I've met somebody! Now Lord, remember my schedule. In about three to four years, some wedding bells need to come out of this!*

Now, I think it is only valid to point out that I never met the man face-to-face. He saw me in church *once*, got my e-mail from my friend, and continued with "let's get to know each other via e-mails" for the next three months. Totally ridiculous, I know! However, back then, I did not fully understand yet that my value came from the love of God for me and *not* the attention of a guy. One invaluable lesson that I have learned while waiting on Immanuel's timing is to truly allow God to fill and tend to every void in your life. As a young girl, I dealt with very low self-esteem and poor body image for so long that I felt I needed to validate myself through good grades, accolades from people, or a boyfriend. At that particular time in life, I viewed marriage as a prize that I had to obtain to feel validated. At nineteen, going on twenty, getting married meant more to me than earning my college degree. I had staked my worth on whether or not I was "marriageable." Well, needless to say, that short-lived "courtship" ended by spring break of 2004, and I found myself back to square one. How does this relate to Hannah? As Penninah kept popping out more babies, Hannah remained childless.

As more friends were getting engaged and married, I remained without companionship.

"And her rival also provoked her severely, to make her miserable, because the Lord had closed her womb. So it was, year by year, when she went up to the house of the Lord, that she provoked her; therefore [Hannah] wept and did not eat."[4] Have you ever had any "Penninahs" in your life? I mean, for real. I'm talking about people in your life who, rather than encouraging you to take heart while you wait patiently for God to bless you, would much rather flaunt what they themselves have already received in front of you and provoke you to the point of tears.

"You know, I think you all need to see if there is anything wrong with Larissa," an older woman once told my mother after Sunday service. "I mean, I just don't understand—she's pretty, she's smart, she loves God, and she goes to church. Why doesn't she have a boyfriend yet? Does she even *like* boys?" This was a true conversation that this woman and countless others would approach my family with. These were my "Penninahs" during my late teens and early twenties. While it seemed that all of my parents' friends were marrying their daughters off at the church, no one could understand why I hadn't been "scooped up" yet. Like Hannah must have felt, these comments stung me like rubbing alcohol on a fresh cut. They pierced my heart because eventually, I started to believe these comments and even began to question the Lord. Was there something wrong with me? If I really had all these good qualities going for me, why was I *still* single? What was *I* doing wrong?

I really empathize with Hannah. She was a woman of God who loved the Lord. I'm sure there were times when her heart ached to understand God's sovereign plan as it related to her long wait to become a mother. Timing, yet again, is imperative to understanding as a kingdom-minded

---

4   1 Samuel 1:7, NKJV.

citizen. What I love the most about Hannah is that never once do we see in the Scriptures that this woman complained to the Lord or lashed out her frustration at her husband, Elkanah. Nor do we see that she tried to manipulate her husband to get her desire for a child met outside of the will of God. We do see, however, that she faithfully went to the temple year after year and waited patiently on the Lord. I believe that the Lord pays very close attention to our *attitude* while we wait. How we behave during the waiting process will determine how long we remain there!

Take an inventory of your own self. How do you respond when you hear of a friend who gets engaged? Do you find yourself dealing with jealousy? How do you respond when another friend gets married? Are you genuinely happy for him or her? Many times I literally threw a temper tantrum when I heard the news of another close friend my age marrying the man of her dreams. However, that is not going through the waiting process *gracefully*. Hannah waited and endured her test of waiting with grace and inner strength from the Lord. God can give you that same strength to endure with grace.

When I look back over my early twenties, I realize that had I been involved in a serious relationship and had gotten married early, I would not have had the privilege to serve the Lord faithfully on my college campus. By the grace of God, I had the honor of leading Bible studies in campus ministry—even serving as campus ministry president for four years. I served young women on my hall as an RA. I worked with the youth at my church. Like Hannah, I just continued being about the Father's business while I waited, not putting my whole life on hold just to wait on a husband. And just like God remembered Hannah and her faithfulness and opened her womb, God will also remember you and your faithfulness to Him while you waited and bless you with the man of your dreams.

Notes from
Hannah's Waiting Process

Confessions of a Bridesmaid

1. What do you believe makes you valuable? Do these things line up with the Word of God?

2. Who were the "Penninahs" in your life?

3. Think about the last time a friend or family member got engaged or married. How did you respond initially?

4. What can you learn from how Hannah waited on God that can help you in your waiting process?

4

While You Wait...

I BELIEVE THAT AS HANNAH WAITED on the Lord with expectancy, God was molding a jewel in her. He was molding her for the task of birthing one of the greatest prophets in the Old Testament, who would later anoint the greatest leader in Israel's history—King David. While she waited, Hannah's heart had to meet a condition. If God had blessed her with a son early on in her marriage, it would probably have been hard for her to have given the child back unto the Lord. She couldn't put her desire for a child above her love and devotion to the Lord. When she went to the temple on that special day and made her vow to the Lord that if the He would bless her with a son, the son would be dedicated unto the Lord for *life*. That is huge!

Ultimately, our desires have to match up with God's desires. We should want what the Father wants. We, as women of God, should not just desire a husband for the sake of having one; we should desire to be the godly help mates that God has called us to be, to walk by the side of the man of God, the Father has for us. We should desire to be excellent godly wives and mothers who raise godly children that God can get glory from and can use in the kingdom. Once Hannah's heart met that condition (and once our hearts do the same), we will see the Lord move on our behalf.

The Lord used Hannah, a special vessel, to birth yet another special vessel. My sisters, be encouraged! Allow God to mold patience, kindness, gracefulness, strength, and all that God needs to do in you during this time. Then your future husband will truly reap the benefit of that "good thing" that the Lord has deposited in you and do what? Obtain *favor* from the Lord because of you! That gets me excited right there! The Scriptures promise us that the Lord truly is good to those who wait.[5]

What is the Lord molding in you during *your* waiting season? What gifts has He deposited in you that need to be birthed *before* God promotes you to the new season of marriage? In hindsight, I realize that my waiting period—though I am still in it now—is my preparation season. In addition to molding me to be a leader to my peers on campus through campus ministry and in the college dorms, the Lord led me to a ministry where my leaders where able to pull out of me the gifts of dance, song, and teaching. I never thought in a million years that God would ever consider me to dance before Him, teach others His Word, or lead songs of worship before Him. However, if I had been wrapped up in a wrong relationship or "putting my life on hold" while a husband came along, I would have completely missed all that the Lord intended to do in and through my life during this season, and I am forever grateful. He knows the plans that He has for us. He knew the plan that He had for Hannah. Hannah did not put her life on hold, waiting for a baby to be born. She continued to serve the Lord *faithfully*. She willingly accepted

---

5   Lamentations 3:25 NKJV.

Immanuel's timing. What dreams or gifts has the Lord deposited in you? What are you doing while *you* wait?

Notes from
While You Wait

Confessions of a Bridesmaid

1. Why do you want to be married? List five of your top reasons.

2. Take a look at your list. Do these reasons match God's design for marriage?

3. List five things you can do now to help you prepare to be a wonderful wife!

4. What dreams and gifts has the Lord deposited in you? Do you know what the calling is on your life?

5

"Rejoice with those who rejoice"

"Larissa, guess what?! I'm *engaged!*" a close friend of mine from college joyfully squealed over the phone. She was so happy; I could feel her enthusiasm and excitement oozing into my end of the receiver. Not that I wasn't delighted to hear such wonderful news, but truth be told, I did feel a pinch of envy. I was having one of those moments.

"Really, God? *Another* one?" was the thought that crossed my mind as I made a mental checklist of the number of engagements and weddings in 2009. Just that year alone, I had been to *five* weddings, and I had learned of the recent engagement of two close friends. The greatest lesson that a woman of God can learn during her season of waiting is that godliness with contentment is *great* gain—truly. It is so easy for the enemy to plant seeds of envy and jealousy in our hearts if we allow him to. My associate pastor once said, "Stop hating!"

Don't believe the lie of the enemy that the Lord is blessing everyone but you—he is a liar! The Word of the Lord tells us that we are to rejoice with those who rejoice and weep with those who weep. Do not allow yourself to fall into the comparison trap—you know the one, when you look at your life and the life of another sister side by side and take inventory. We have all been guilty of this at one point, when we compare how things in our life just don't seem to measure up to another person. God has promised that "He who has begun a good work in you is faithful to complete it, until the day of Jesus Christ."[6]

Can I be transparent? There have been times when I have had to ask the Lord for forgiveness for being envious of friends who had been blessed with what I am still waiting on the Lord for, which in this case is marriage. I would present this long laundry list to God of reasons why I should be married by now. "Well, God, I love you; God, I'm faithful; Well, God, I've waited long enough; But, God, she and I are both saved and active in ministry. Why did you bless *her* with a husband and not me yet?" And blah, blah, blah! After this long whining session I had with the Lord, I was very ashamed when I realized how childish I was acting and how selfish a perspective I had. Thank you, Jesus, for mercy! Who are *we* to question the Lord on who He is going to bless now and who He is going to bless later? Our job is certainly not to compare our lives to another sister's life. God is working on a master plan for *your* life as well as your sister in the Lord.

Ask the Lord to really perfect contentment in your heart and to uproot and totally eradicate any seeds of jealousy and envy in your heart. I can assure you that if you are a woman of God about her Father's business, who is constantly seeking to be in the will of God and walking

---

6   Philippians 1:6 NKJV.

in love, then you won't have time to be comparing your life to someone else's because there is much to do in the kingdom!

I challenge you: every time a close friend or sister gets engaged or married, purpose in your heart to rejoice *with* her and *for* her! Tell yourself, "God, if you are blessing my sister, then that *must* mean my blessing is on the way too." So, stop hatin'! While you wait, learn to rejoice over the blessings of others.

Notes from

Rejoice with Those Who Rejoice

Confessions of a Bridesmaid

1. Have you ever been guilty of the "Comparison Trap"? Describe one example of this in your life.

2. Examine your heart right now. Do you struggle with bitterness and jealously in your heart? Why?

3. Why is jealously not only displeasing to God, but also very dangerous to the believer?

4. By choosing to rejoice over another sister or friend rather than being jealous, how do you think that will make it easier to wait on God?

6

Faith to Trust His Timing

LADIES, THE ISSUE OF FAITH DURING the waiting process is one that is necessary to explore. The Word of God says that without faith, it is impossible to please Him. All too often, when it comes to single, saved women, it can be difficult to trust God with this area of our lives. There are some days when I ask the Lord, "When will my husband, the man you have selected for me, *ever* find me? Does he even *exist*? Is it really worth holding out for him?" I once read that women exercise their faith in God (as it relates to marriage) by waiting to be found. If that is the case, we need to revisit the character and nature of the one who promises good things to those who wait patiently on Him.

First, we serve an almighty, all-powerful God! If God Almighty could cause the Red Sea to part, if He could cause manna to rain from heaven, if He could create our entire universe in a matter of six days, surely God can bless you with a mate, if that is your heart's desire. God is our Jehovah Jireh, our Provider. He promises that He is able to supply *all* of our needs according to His riches and glory. I think sometimes we forget that God not only sees us as His friends and His instruments to use in the earth, but God sees us as His daughters—our daddy is the King! What father, especially a king, would not be more than happy to lavish his precious daughter with all she needs? If God cares about the well-being of a *sparrow,* how much more valuable to Him are you? He is very aware of the deepest longings of our hearts, and He knows exactly *what* we need *when* we need it. Use this time to fall in love with Father. Seek His face and not His hand. Really get to know the Lord on a level that is intimate and personal. I promise you this: He is able to fill every void, hurt, and painful place in our hearts with His love. Never allow yourself to believe that a relationship with someone can fill that void. Relationships are wonderful, especially if they are God-ordained. But desire the sweeter relationship—a deeper love for Abba, Father.

I had an experience where I was faced with the choice to really trust that God is able to provide. I had to believe that He was able to bless me with what my heart desired. I had to choose to *not* settle." I had to dismiss the fear that He would not come through and thus give in to pressure from family and friends. It was an experience that I know drew me closer to the Father.

It was the summer of 2007, just a few months after my first serious relationship had ended. I can remember how this window was such a delicate time for me. God was still mending my heart, and I was in the early stages of the healing process. I was also in "guys *suck*" mode for that time as well. It was hard on my family to watch me endure the aftermath of the breakup, so in their eyes, it was time for me to move on with my life and embark upon some new "romantic endeavors." Let me be the first to say that jumping into another relationship while your heart is still mending doesn't speed up the healing process. More often than not, it can be a detriment. So make sure that you have given God all the time necessary to heal your heart.

A godly couple who have been friends of the family for a long time suggested that I meet their nephew, who they felt would be a good match for me. He was eleven years older than me and was a doctor. (Hello!) The only things that we had in common were that we were both Haitian and we both spoke Spanish fluently. After meeting the gentleman, I knew right from the start that this would *not* work. He went to church but didn't really show the fruit that was evidence of a relationship with the Lord. I just did not sense in my spirit that he had the godly qualities I was looking for in a husband and the future father of my children someday. Ladies, listen to me when I say this: do not settle! If you have your *own* personal relationship with the Lord, He will reveal to you whether or not a relationship a brother desires to initiate with you will be fruitful in your life.

Remember that when I met him, I was twenty-three, and according to the cultural timetable my community had set up, I was *severely* behind schedule. To my family, that dreaded biological clock was ticking. So this guy became the "you better catch this one while you can" situation. For the next six months, he was relentlessly pursuing me, while on the other side, my family and the family friends were desperately trying to persuade me to marry him. At this point, everyone around me wanted to hear some wedding bells.

Regardless of the opinions, feelings, and perspectives of others, God is in control. Not only that, but He is the master matchmaker. There were times when I was so tempted to just throw in the towel and give in to the pressure to marry this guy. I could have given in to the lie of the enemy that kept ringing in my ear, "God has forgotten about you anyway. You might as well grab this one while you can." But that would have been seriously settling and not exercising my faith that God is able to do exceedingly, abundantly more than what I could ever ask or think. Much to the dismay of my family and that particular family friend, I did not marry this man. However, God did reveal to everyone later on that he was not what he seemed anyway. He ended up not being a genuine person after all. I thank God for giving me the strength and discernment not to give in and settle.

God is so good and so desperately wants to blow your mind with how good He can be to those who wait on Him. I encourage you: please do not rob God of the joy of blessing you with someone who is exceedingly, abundantly *more* than you could ask or think. Don't settle for Bozo! Trust that God, in His perfect timing, will bring to you your Boaz!

Notes from

Faith to Trust His Timing

Confessions of a Bridesmaid

1. Read Hebrews 11:1-6. In your own words, describe *faith*.

2. Why does our faith please God so much?

Confessions of a Bridesmaid

3. Have you ever "settled" in order to be in a relationship? What was the outcome?

4. Read the story of Ruth in the Bible. List five qualities that you observe in Boaz that made him an excellent husband.

7

Being a Bridesmaid 101

I ONCE READ A BUMPER STICKER that said: "Girls don't go to college to find their husbands; they go to college to find their bridesmaids." As cute as this thought was, it holds a lot of truth. In every young woman's life, the group of girls that she selects to be her bridesmaids really makes up the most important people in her life as she prepares for her wedding day—other than her hubby, of course!

So where did the concept of bridesmaids originate from anyway? The idea of a bride having bridesmaids actually dates back to ancient Roman days. It was required that ten witnesses (five young men and five young women) be present at the wedding ceremony. The ancient Romans believed that evil spirits would try to wreak havoc on the new couple and attempt to sabotage the wedding. Therefore, in an effort to "confuse" these spirits, the bridesmaids and groomsmen (as we call them today) would dress identically to the bride and groom, so that the spirits could not tell who was getting married.[7] However, I am sure down through the course of history, some bride thought, "Heck, I'm the star of this show!" and thus demanded that the bridesmaids wear a different dress from the bride. You can't outshine the bride!

But seriously, what exactly *is* the role of a bridesmaid? In all the times that I have been a bridesmaid, it was my duty to purchase the dress (regardless of my *personal* opinion of it) and all the matching accessories; get my nails done; do my hair; attend all the practices and the rehearsal dinner; purchase both a bridal shower and wedding gift; get to the church in the limousine *on time;* stand throughout the entire ceremony (in high heel shoes!) and attend the wedding reception. Now that's some love!

However, this is not to complain about the expenses and responsibility. Being a bridesmaid really is an opportunity to lovingly serve the bride-to-be in all the preparation leading up to the wedding day. These things relay to your friend how much you care about her on her special day, as her bridesmaid. The bride selecting you means that out of all of her friends and acquaintances, she has valued your friendship so much that she desires you to be a part of this special moment in her life.

Furthermore, the most important lesson in being a bridesmaid is that it is not about *you.* If there was ever a time when selflessness was called for, it is in being a bridesmaid. I have always had in the back of my mind that when I become a bride, I would want my bridesmaids to be just as faithful and supportive of me as I have been for my friends. Just seeing the number of my friends who have already gotten married, planning a wedding is no walk in the park! Between addressing invitations, finding a church, trying to accommodate lodging for the

---

7   Andres, Cath. "Bridesmaid duties in modern Italian and Ancient Roman weddings. *http://www.explore-italian-culture.com/bridesmaid-duties.html* (accessed March 3, 2010).

bride's family and the groom's, visiting florists, and wedding dress shopping, a supportive team of bridesmaids makes this all the more memorable and makes the process go so much smoother.

However, what I can say is that the most important thing a woman of God can do as a bridesmaid for another woman of God is to keep her in prayer. I talked about how the ancient Romans instituted the role of bridesmaids and groomsmen as witnesses to the covenant relationship that took place between a man and a woman on their wedding day. I heard a pastor say at the wedding of two of my dearest friends that a wedding is not just a simple ceremony but a *testimony*. We are witnesses to the love that the Creator has put in their hearts for each other as they pledge their lives to each other before the Lord. As you stand by the bride on her day, use this as an opportunity to lift up this new couple before the Lord. It is an opportunity to intercede on their behalf for the guidance of the Lord for every day of their lives together. It is a chance to pray for the children who will come forth as the fruit of their union. Even after the wedding bells have stopped ringing and all of the guests have gone home, continue to be a supportive role model in the life of the new wife. I am so blessed now to be the godmother for one of my dearest friends, who offered me the privilege to walk in her wedding. Not only was I a witness to her and her husband's testimony of love to each other, but now, I now play a special role in the life of their son—I'm his godmother. What an honor! So ladies, truly serve as a bridesmaid with great joy. You will be planting seeds toward your own special day.

Notes from

Being a Bridesmaid 101

Confessions of a Bridesmaid

1. In your opinion, what are the three most important qualities every bridesmaid should possess? Did you emulate these qualities the last time you were a bridesmaid? How you serve another sister on her special day will be seeds (good or bad) you plant towards your *own* wedding day.

2. What do you like the *most* about being a bridesmaid?

Confessions of a Bridesmaid

3. What is your *least* favorite thing about being a bridesmaid?

4. One day, it will be your turn to be the blushing bride. Describe your dream wedding.

8

Memories of a Bridesmaid

As enjoyable as it is to be a bridesmaid, including all of the sacrifices that have to be made to help make your friend's day memorable, you can't forget all of the bloopers that happen behind the scenes to make the wedding day go as smoothly as possible. The following are my most memorable experiences as a bridesmaid. I hope they make you smile.

THE JAPANESE BRIDESMAID

It was a few weeks before my eighteenth birthday, and I had accepted the call to be a bridesmaid for a sister at church. At the time, I was not thrilled that the wedding was so close to my birthday, because the funds that I could have used for my birthday were now being funneled to purchase items for the wedding. Then, of course, there was the hairdo … I looked like a Japanese princess. I remember that she wanted all of us to have our hair up in a tight bun, with bangs. The bun was so tight that I literally felt that I had a face lift in the hair salon. All that was missing were our matching kimonos. Putting all personal opinions about the coiffeur aside, the wedding was beautiful. The happy couple is still married and has two beautiful children.

WEDDING BELLS ON CHRISTMAS DAY

This was probably the most unusual bridesmaid experience, because it came on Christmas Day. Evidently, this particular bride wanted a *husband* under her Christmas tree that year. The cousin of a friend of mine needed a replacement bridesmaid, because at the last minute, one of her bridesmaids bailed on her. (Not good bridesmaid etiquette!) So, of course, I agreed to step in and help save the day for this bride—it was Christmas, after all. We all had to wear what I like to call my "Ice Princess" dress, which was an icy blue color. It was freezing that day, and the dress had spaghetti straps. Now that's what I call a sacrifice! Nevertheless, it was a simple yet very nice, intimate wedding. Although I did not know the bride personally in this case, it really did feel good to assist her on this special occasion.

RUNAWAY LIMO?

This story takes the cake for being the *funniest* bridesmaid story. My friend and I were waiting at the house of a sister who had agreed to do all of the bridesmaids' hair for the wedding. My friend's mother was the matron of honor for the occasion. Now, for the record, we *were* already finished with our hair and ready to leave to go to the church. As a bridesmaid, you can expect at least one thing to go wrong on the bride's big day. Your job is to make sure to handle the problem with as little commotion as possible so she is not stressed. To make a long story short, the limo driver picked up the matron of honor and *left* the two of us at the house. The wedding was supposed to start in about thirty minutes, and we were still stuck on the other side of town. So we had to find someone to come and pick us up and drive us to the church.

Picture this: we were two frantic bridesmaids running into the church with our hair and makeup done. We were in jeans and with our dresses in hand. We ended up having to get dressed at the church. It's hilarious now, but definitely not then!

THE GOLD DRESS

I had some negative feelings toward this particular dress, mainly because it was a dress meant for a *junior* bridesmaid. Because I looked so much younger than my other friends who also walked in the wedding and was a little less developed, the sister getting married just assumed that I was younger and had me wear the junior bridesmaid version of the dress. Remember how I mentioned that as a bridesmaid, you have to expect the unexpected and keep everything going as smoothly as possible? This was one of those times. One of the ushers had a horrible dress fiasco—black eyeliner spilled all over her dress as she was putting on makeup. As a result, she couldn't participate in the wedding. At the last minute, we were one groomsman short, so I had to double up with another bridesmaid and her partner. It was really a sight to see: one groomsman with two bridesmaids on either side. A lot of mishaps happened that day, too. No one could locate the canes and top hats for the groomsmen; one bridesmaid lost her shoe. There was a lot of stress going on behind the scenes. But like every good bridesmaid, you just have to keep a smile, stay positive, and remember: it's not about you!

THE KEY LIME MERMAID DRESS

Every bridesmaid has worn, at least once, "The Dress." I am talking about the bridesmaid dress that you want to rip up into shreds because it is so hideous. And no, you will *never* wear it again for the public eye to see. This dress truly took the prize. Unlike the other weddings where I was a personal friend of the bride, I was a good friend of the groom this time. My dad's closest friend was getting married and wanted me to walk in his wedding. Since he has no children of his own yet, he has always viewed my brothers and me as his own kids. So I was so honored to be a part of his special day. I had the privilege of meeting his new wife a few months before the wedding. She is a beautiful godly woman and has such a fun-loving spirit. One of the blessings that happened during this wedding was that for *once,* I did not have to pay a dime for my dress. My dad's friend, the groom, took care of it for me. Another interesting aspect about this wedding is that instead of purchasing a dress from a bridal shop, this bride had a friend who was willing to sew all the dresses for all of her bridesmaids. So I gave her my measurements a few months ahead of time and went about my business. She wanted a multicolored wedding, so each bride would wear the same dress, only in a different color. When she had asked me my color preference, I told her that my favorite color was purple.

The month of the wedding finally rolled around and it was time for me to get the final fitting for my dress. When I finally saw the dress, I thought I was going to have a heart attack; the dress was *not* purple, but rather a bright *lime* green. The bottom was a mermaid shape, with a matching jacket, complete with flared sleeves, flowers surrounding the collar, and silver buttons. My heart sank down to my knees. I could not dare show any sign of discontentment with the final product, because the bride was so excited and happy. How could I possibly burst her bubble? All I kept thinking was, Lord, *I have to take pictures in this?* However, at the end of the day, after I had pushed aside my personal feelings about wearing the dress, the wedding was indeed beautiful, and everyone had a wonderful time.

Notes from

Memories of a Bridesmaid

Confessions of a Bridesmaid

1. What is your best memory of being a bridesmaid?

2. Describe the funniest thing that has ever happened to you as a bridesmaid.

Confessions of a Bridesmaid

3. Describe your *worst* bridesmaid dress

4. What is your favorite part at any wedding?

9
Waiting in Purity

I AM TWENTY-FIVE YEARS OLD, AND I am still a virgin. In fact, I have never even been kissed by a guy. As sexually explicit as our society has become, this confession would cause most jaws to drop. This is not in any way tooting my own horn. If it was not for the grace of God, I would have had a much different story. However, I believe that this issue of purity is very important to discuss. The Lord desires and even makes it very plain in His Word about remaining sexually pure before marriage.

Now, if your upbringing was anything like mine, growing up, the message about sex from the pulpit was pretty clear: "Don't have sex until you are married!" This was as far as the teaching about sexuality in the church went. I have come to learn that girls, particularly in a Haitian household, hold the honor for the family. Growing up, when I saw or heard of girls my age who got pregnant out of wedlock, the level of shame that others put on these girls was so unbearable that my thinking was, "If *I* ever got pregnant out of wedlock, my family would

67

flat out *disown* me!" This was how serious it was for a young woman to remain pure until marriage.

The pressure was even higher for me, since I am the eldest and the only girl in my immediate family. Dating was strictly forbidden for me until I graduated from college (so much for *that*). My grandmother always used to say this old Haitian proverb: "Guys and girls are like matches and gasoline." So, when I hit sixteen and wanted a boyfriend like the rest of my friends, my mom's response was: "A boyfriend?! Your *books* are your boyfriend." Well, there was my answer.

Before I left to go to college, several people I knew were very surprised to hear that I was going away to live on campus. Many parents in my community were very apprehensive to send their daughters off to live on a college campus because of the stories of how young ladies would go away to school and come home pregnant. So when the news spread that I was indeed going away to school, coming from such a strict upbringing and sheltered life, the responses that I received were less than encouraging and not at all what I had expected to hear. "*Larissa* is going away to college?! That girl has never had a day of liberty in her *life*—college is gonna turn her out."

So before I had even stepped foot on UGA's campus, there were those who were already expecting and even waiting for me to give in to sexual compromise and all of the other temptations that college campuses offer—but thanks be to God! When I look back over my years in college, it makes me love the Father all the more for His keeping power. For a long time, I used to be ashamed of my testimony. I wasn't the girl who drank, smoked, went to the club, or slept around. All I knew was church. Because I did grow up sheltered, I felt that my testimony was weak compared to another whom God had delivered and restored from those things. I did not feel that I was qualified to even witness to someone who had gone through that kind of life. I felt that I would just be looked upon as the typical "church girl."

However, it was not until I graduated from college that I realized how *awesome* God's grace and mercy were on my life. Although my testimony was not a horror story of crazy college life, which is expected and the norm, my testimony is this: you *can* go away to college and be kept *from* the crazy college life only by the grace of God! I am very grateful that the Lord would even surround me with young adults who were passionate and sold out to the Lord, which encouraged me and proved to me that you can live a life of holiness unto the Lord while you are young. Holiness is not a bad word—it's what the Lord expects from His children.

A young woman's purity is not just a treasure she has to keep for her husband one day, but it is something that will please the heart of God. It is something of immense value. Even if my husband *never* comes (although I have faith that he will), my heart's desire is to offer before God a pure heart, a pure mind, and a pure body. Do you know why God instructs us to come before Him with clean hands and a pure heart? It is because something that is pure is free from any and all contaminants. Because God is holy, we cannot come before Him just any kind of way. He is the King of Kings! Just like the priests in the Old Testament were required to literally bathe themselves in the bronze laver before they could even enter into the tabernacle, it's the same way that we are to allow God to cleanse us as well.

What kind of things can contaminate your heart, mind, and body as it relates to sexual purity? Fornication is the obvious one. God purposed for sex to be enjoyed within the covenant relationship found between a *husband and wife*. In other words, unless that brother has put a ring on your finger and you have said "I do," there should be no sexual activity going on between you and a man who is not your husband. When sex is done within the boundaries that God has established, then is it pleasing to Him.

However, sex outside of marriage is not the only thing that can contaminate our hearts, minds, and bodies. All sexual immorality (pornography, masturbation, etc.) can cause us to compromise our sexual purity before the Lord. Our bodies as single women (and men) of God belong to Him, and anything we do with our bodies that results in us not feeling pure before God afterward breaks His heart. Ladies, please hear me on this. Our God is so good, so loving, and so *merciful* toward us, that it would behoove us to want to live a life of purity and holiness just because of who He is to us. The Scripture "beseeches" us, which in other words means begs us to offer our bodies up to the Lord, as living sacrifices, holy and pleasing unto God as our reasonable (meaning it's the *least* that we can do) act of service. The Lord Jesus Christ was beaten beyond recognition. He was mocked, spat upon, and endured the humiliation of dying on a cross, the punishment only criminals received, for *you*. On that cross, He died for the sins of every person who has slept around. He took upon himself the guilt associated with self-pleasure. He took upon himself the sin of everyone who has been lured in by the lust associated with pornography. He has even taken away the shame, hurt, and pain that comes from rape and molestation, things that were probably no fault of your own. He died just for you and me so that we would not have to bear the burdens associated with these sins. He died so we could be free to live a life of holiness. Every drop of His blood that was shed has washed us pure and made us white as snow.

You may be reading this book today, and maybe you are saved and love God, but you find yourself struggling with sexual purity. Perhaps you were violated and taken advantage of at a young age and find yourself dealing with the issue of purity. The enemy loves to keep things in the dark, and the longer you suffer in silence, the longer he has something he *thinks* he can hang over your head. Make a liar out of the devil today! Don't struggle with it alone. I encourage you find someone who loves God, someone you can talk to and get the deliverance you need. Find someone who will pray for you and touch and agree with you that all that the enemy stole from you as it relates to your purity has been restored in Jesus Christ. God desires to set you free from the pain of the past. Most importantly, being filled with the Holy Spirit will give you the power to live the overcoming life, not just in this area but *every* area of your life. Make the commitment today, if you've not done so already, to live a life of purity and holiness before Jesus Christ, our Bridegroom.

Notes from

Waiting in Purity

Confessions of a Bridesmaid

1. Purity starts first in your mind. Memorize Philippians 4:8. If you find yourself battling with impure thoughts, use this scripture as a filter. Is what you're thinking first *pure*? Lovely? True? Or good report? If the answer is no, replace those thoughts with the Word of God.

2. "I will set nothing wicked before my eyes" (Psalm 101:3). Think of the types of movies, television shows or internet sites that you are watching. If they are making you compromise your purity, make the decision to stop today.

3. The Word God warns us to not, "stir up nor awaken love until it pleases" (Song of Solomon 8:4). This is a charge to us to remain sexually pure before marriage. Sexually immorality is *not* just limited to sex. Masturbation, pornography, etc are also ways that can "awaken" love before time. If you find yourself struggling in this area, God wants you to deliver you and set you free so you can live a life of purity. Talk with a trusted leader in your church or a parent that can pray with you as you start a life of purity today.

4. When the temptation to compromise your purity, the Bible makes it very clear as to what to do: *FLEE!* (2 Timothy 2:22). In other words, run away from that situation! Make a list of some practical things you can do to flee from a situation that would compromise your life of purity unto the Lord.

10

Lessons I've Learned about Dating

IF YOU ARE UP TO DATE with pop culture, then you are probably very familiar with the reality shows, *The Bachelor* and *The Bachelorette*. I have watched a few episodes of these shows, and I have come to realize a few things about dating that the world not only teaches but advocates. First, in order for you to find "the one," it is imperative to date several different people to get a better feel for the type of person you would like to marry. And if you're on this show, you date several people *at the same time. What the heck?* Now, I'm pretty old-fashioned, and in my opinion, it is not emotionally sound for a man or a woman to engage in multiple romantic relationships—well, not in the kingdom, anyway. Essentially, if one relationship goes sour, you are carrying emotional baggage from one to the next. However, the world advocates to the young woman, "date around"; "put yourself out there"; "you only live once." That's like saying you need to put your hand on a hot stove multiple times in order to know that fire burns!

Another thing I have observed about the world's perspective on dating is the obsession with "romantic love." Please don't get me wrong; I believe that any godly marriage needs romance. In fact, God is the author of love and romance. (Just read Song of Solomon if you don't believe me.) However, the media has implanted in the minds of young women from childhood through movies like *Cinderella, Snow White,* and *Sleeping Beauty,* just to name a few, to seek out this "happily ever after" ending. It puts an unrealistic perspective on finding a mate. In my adult life, I have only been in two romantic relationships, which were both short-lived. Therefore, I am trusting God that the next relationship that I am in leads to marriage. It's time to stop the games, the foolishness, and the relationships that have no real purpose. I don't believe the lie that you have to date five, seven, or twenty-five people to find a wife or to be found by a husband. God is the ultimate matchmaker, and when He leads, it will keep you from unnecessary heartache and grief. If you are a young woman of God reading this and have found yourself in a relationship that has no real purpose, I encourage you to wait for God's best. You are worth it!

With all that said, although I am not married yet, I still feel that the following lessons I have learned about this subject have served for me as an example of what a courtship is *not* supposed to look like. I pray that these insights bless you before you enter into a courtship that God has ordained.

LESSON #1: MEN ARE THE INITIATORS; NOT YOU

King Solomon, the richest and wisest man in history, wrote this God-inspired proverb that will set a lot of ladies free: "He that finds a wife finds a good thing and obtains favor from the Lord."[8] First of all, the Word of God makes it plain as day; the *man* is supposed to do the finding, or in other words the seeking out. Ladies, it is totally out of order for *you* to be chasing after some guy. Men will do whatever it takes to get what they truly desire. Just look at Jacob and Rachel. This guy worked fourteen *years* for this girl, but it only felt like a few days because of his love for her. That lets me know that not only did Rachel have it going *on*, but Jacob represents the type of man that we should desire pursuing our hand.

I had an experience where I dated a brother in church, and before we even started dating, it was pretty obvious that we were growing in our attraction to one another. While we were friends, I knew that I had liked him and was pretty sure that he reciprocated the feeling. However, my mistake, which you ladies need to avoid, is that instead of me waiting for *him* to voice his intentions, I pulled it out of him. It is not our place to give a guy some help in pursuing us. If he does not see you for the jewel that you already are, then it is certainly not *your* job to remind him.

In that same vein, how a young man attempts to pursue you also plays a huge role. At this point in my life, I will not tolerate any guy trying to initiate a relationship with me via text, Facebook, MySpace, Twitter, Skype, telephone, or any other form of technology that comes out! Been there and done that! A man who is serious about a particular job position would not conduct an interview with a great company via text or a telephone, right? Likewise, it is not acceptable for a brother to approach a young woman he desires in the same manner. Some things are better done face to face. I firmly believe that a man should approach a young woman he is interested in pursuing, with integrity, honesty, and **clear intentions**. This leads to another important lesson.

---

8   Proverbs 18:22 NKJV.

LESSON #2: "TO PURSUE OR NOT TO PURSUE?"

"I've had to learn this lesson the hard way—one too many times." Now, it has become my soapbox. Before a guy approaches you ladies, it is best that he first gets clearance from the Lord and then does his "homework" concerning how and when to express his interest in you. Just as it is important for women to wait on God's timing, it is equally important for men—the priests created in God's image—to know when it is the right time to begin a *purposeful* relationship that will lead to a God-honoring marriage. I mentioned early in this book about my first dating experience with a brother in my church while in college. In hindsight, everything truly *is* 20/20 as the saying goes. Looking back, I realize now that there were several things lacking that made this young man unprepared to pursue *anybody* at that point in his life.

So, what are some things you are to look for when you find yourself being pursued? First, realize that when the spiritual and the natural are both in order, that makes an irresistible combination. What attracted me the most to this young man was his love for the Lord, his spiritual maturity, and his commitment to ministry. All of these are wonderful qualities to admire in a man of God—but they are certainly not the only things. The Genesis account of Adam and Eve tells me that God first gave Adam a home, a job, and *then* a companion. Notice the order here: God will not release you to a man to be his helpmate when he has no home for you to live in or the means to provide for you. Likewise, with this particular brother, although things were in order spiritually, in the natural, things were not quite in order yet. One thing that always strikes me when I read about Adam and Eve is that God created a man and a woman; *not* a boy and a girl. Therefore, *boys* don't get married, nor do they pursue wives.

When we started dating, I was in my fourth year of college. I was finally at the age where I could date, and I viewed this relationship as one that would lead to marriage. At the time, there were several red flags that were clouded by my rose-colored glasses (we'll discuss this a little later) that were obvious to others but not to me. A few months into the relationship, we started making plans toward marriage. However, neither one of us was ready to be married—not financially, not emotionally, not spiritually, and not mentally. As much as we desired to be a married couple, we simply were *not* ready. And because God created the man to lead the relationship, this brother still needed to mature in some areas before plunging headfirst into a courtship with the intent of marriage. I believe that God is pleased with *order*. A young man who decides to court a young woman but is not ready in the natural or the spiritual is out of order.

Let me say this—you need to be honest with yourself when making the decision to engage in a courtship with someone. If you are a young woman with goals, high standards, and a vision for your life, but the guy who desires to pursue you is not on the same page, I don't care if he can pray fire from heaven—it will not be a good choice for you!

LESSON #3: TAKE THE ROSE COLORED GLASSES *OFF!*

In 1 Corinthians 13, by the inspiration of the Holy Spirit, Paul eloquently pens the most famous chapter on love. However, nowhere in my Bible have I found that "love is blind." This age-old phrase in American culture has been used as a crutch, unfortunately, for many people to dive headfirst into relationships and marriages with no thorough evaluation of the other person. The Bible says, "Blessed is the man you *choose* and causes to approach you. That he may dwell in your courts and shall be satisfied with the goodness of your house."[9] Ladies, although men are the initiators, we have the task of either choosing to accept or decline a young man's desire to pursue us. Dr. Gary Chapman, the author of the bestselling book, *The 5 Love Languages Singles Edition* really gives an excellent description of the "in love" phenomenon that we all experience when we first engage in a relationship with someone. Dr. Chapman writes:

> The experience of "falling in love" is not a foundation for a happy marriage. It is highly possible to be "in love" with someone you should not marry … on the other hand, the "tingles" may develop into the emotional obsession I am calling the experience of "falling in love." None of this requires much effort or thought. All you did was show up, and the emotions took over. However, a marital relationship designed to last a lifetime requires more than these euphoric, obsessive feelings. (p 159)[10]

This obsessive stage normally lasts between one to two years, Dr. Chapman also mentions in his book. In my little "rose-colored" stage, I was clearly living on cloud nine every waking second. I will say that it is definitely *not* a wise choice to make any drastic decisions during this stage. During this window of time, it is difficult to see the forest from the trees.

I remember that we started courting in September 2006; by October, we were acting like a little married couple. By December, we were already talking about marriage, looking at engagement rings and furniture for a home—crazy, right? All the while, I'm not doing my homework by asking questions such as: What are your goals and plans *after* college? *How* are we gonna pay for these things? and more.

---

9   Psalm 65:4 NKJV.
10   Chapman, 159.

Falling in love is a wonderful thing; however, do not allow yourself to be so infatuated with another person that you lose all common sense! Marriage is lifelong commitment, a covenant established by God. Therefore, take the rose-colored glasses off long enough to ask the right questions, do your homework, and see the other person for who they really are.

LESSON #4: AGE *IS* JUST A NUMBER … RIGHT?

I realize that this next paragraph may hit a nerve with a few of you—but that's all right! I have had this discussion with numerous people, and the opinions vary from person to person. My mother always taught me that it was better for me to date or marry someone who was a few years older than me. And based on the experiences I've had, where I have dated guys who were younger than me, I've come to realize that "Momma knows best." I think it is important for a young lady to be very honest about whether she is comfortable dating someone who is much older or much younger than she is. Not that this is a blanket statement for all younger men, however with age does come life experience and wisdom. One thing I have observed when I dated a younger guy is that I was always just a few steps ahead. It made me feel guilty at times; I felt that I came across as intimidating because I was further along in some areas. In fact, one relationship with a brother I dated ended simply because we weren't on "the same page" of life.

When the Scriptures talk about how believers are not to be unequally yoked to nonbelievers, I believe it doesn't just stop there. Two believers could be unequally yoked simply because they are not on the same page of life. As a woman of God, no one should make you feel bad because you are about your Father's business and you have a vision for your life. Now, I know a lot of young brothers in Christ who not only love God but have a clear sense of what God has called them to do *and are doing it!* However, there are some brothers in the kingdom who may love God but are not mature enough or in a place where they are ready to pursue marriage. Ultimately, the final decision falls in the hands of the young lady and God. If you find yourself interested in a brother but are not sure of level of maturity in comparison to yours, it would be wise for you to observe, ask questions, and seek the Lord for yourself about whether or not he could be a suitable husband. I mentioned earlier, **little boys don't get married**. Men make the decision to marry, and these need to be men who are not only lovers of Jesus but realize what it all entails to be somebody's husband.

LESSON # 5: WHAT TO DO WHEN YOU LIKE HIM "MORE THAN JUST A FRIEND"

Growing up, I loved hearing my parents and my grandmother share with me old Haitian proverbs; every culture has their own. One of the most memorable proverbs from one of my favorite Haitian movies, *I Love You, Anne,* is found in the scene where the father and his daughter, Anne, have the "boys" talk. When he realizes that a certain young man is pursuing his daughter, he demands to know who he is. Anne responds, "He's a friend, Dad. Just a friend." Her father retorts back, "Oh yeah? Just *friends?* Boys and girls can't just remain friends. They are like matches and gasoline."[11]

The essence behind this proverb is that it is virtually impossible to stop an attraction from developing between the sexes. Regardless of who is attracted to whom first, sparks will fly. That's how God created us to be. One piece of advice that I can share with all you single ladies (and single men who may read this) is to be careful to guard your heart as it relates to your friendship with the opposite sex. What I mean is that it is

---

11 Tessier, Silvio. *I Love You, Anne.* DVD. Richard Senecal. Haiti: Haiti, 2003

very easy to develop a form of emotional dependency with the member of the opposite sex, even if you are not in a dating relationship. I will never forget the words of wisdom one of my campus ministry leaders gave us during our first year of college. He warned us that it was not a good idea to spend substantial amounts of time with a member of the opposite sex on the phone late at night or prolonged periods of time alone. Why? Late at night, we have a tendency to put our guard down. Come on, you're sleepy! Of course, I had to learn this the hard way.

A few months after graduating from college, I started to develop a friendship with another brother who had recently joined our church. Over time, our thirty-minute conversations grew to three, four, sometimes five hours on the phone every day. After a while, I did begin developing romantic feelings for him and began to question the true status of this "friendship." A young man does not merit my time and attention after a certain time in the evening because 1) he's *not* my husband, and 2) what do we possibly have to talk about at *2:00* in the morning? There is nothing wrong with having a brother as a close friend. However, be advised that if the amount of time that you spend together begins to mimic the same amount of time that you would invest in a romantic relationship, it could lead to the development of romantic feelings—believe me, I know.

When you find yourself good friends with a brother (who you may also be attracted to) carefully limit the amount of time that you spend with him on the phone or by yourselves. If he is really a man of God, he will realize that it is important for you to guard your heart. Until he voices his intentions, he also needs to understand that he is not entitled to all of your time and attention! When you both begin to develop those "I like this person more than just as a friend" feelings, first take these feelings to God. Second, recruit the help of an accountability partner, preferably a godly married couple who has been down this road before. And of course, your pastor, the man or woman that God has covering you, is always an excellent person to seek out for wise counsel. The bottom line is that with any relationship in the kingdom, platonic or not, you need to treat the other person with care, because he or she belongs to God. When a child of God breaks another child of God's heart because of carelessness or selfishness, this really breaks God's heart, too.

LESSON #6: GIVE GOD TIME TO HEAL YOUR HEART

I had never experienced heartache until after my first relationship went sour. It is a part of life that, unfortunately, we all have to deal with. However, this experience really taught me how much of a comforter God was and how close He truly is to the brokenhearted. The days following the breakup were the hardest days I'd had to face up until this point in life. Not only did he end relationship the day *before* my final exams (great timing, right?), but we were still a part of the same ministry until he relocated a few months later. So you can imagine the immense awkwardness, pain, and discomfort there was on both sides after it was all said and done. I truly thank God for the grace to endure that difficult season, because it would have been easier to remain bitter and hurt. However, what helped through all of it was the constant reminder that, "I am still in the kingdom. I cannot handle this situation like someone in the world would handle this. God, despite how I feel, I need you to help me respond to this in a way that you will be pleased."

I not only struggled with feelings of rejection, anger, and hurt for quite some time, but I also experienced many feelings of inadequacy. For months, I analyzed every angle of the relationship. *Perhaps I could have done things differently,* went through my mind for months. Then, *Why was I not good enough?* followed soon after. Because he did not handle my heart in an honorable way, it caused me to take longer to heal. I found myself putting up a wall around my heart, for fear of ever being vulnerable again. It took about three years to fully recover.

The biggest obstacle that I had to overcome during the healing process was first admitting that my heart was still hurting. Sometimes people, especially women, can say that they are "over" a situation. However, God has a way to reveal our heart's true condition to ourselves. I realized that I was still harboring unforgiveness toward this brother. I was angry at how things were handled, and I felt for a long time that I never received the closure I needed to move on.

However, one day I had a friend who sent me a link to a YouTube video for a song entitled, "A Heart that Forgives" by Kevin LeVarr. When I heard that song, it felt like a huge weight fell off of my heart. It was then that I finally asked God to help me let go of this pain and anger I had been holding on to and give it to Him. That same day, in the form of a letter, I finally expressed how I had been feeling to this brother, after about two years, and forgave him. Since then, I have experienced such a peace and a freedom to really leave this in the past and move on with life. It is very important that you take the time to heal from a broken relationship and do not jump into another one until you are healed.

God desires that we not walk around wounded and broken, but free. It is very easy to put up a wall and walk in fear of opening your heart up again to another person. But I want to encourage you today not to walk in fear. God has not given us a spirit of fear but a spirit of power, love, and a sound mind! I had been crippled in my mind for a long time because of the fear of getting hurt again. But I am very thankful that God can restore a broken heart, and He can restore your heart if you allow Him. One bad experience does not need to hinder you from experiencing a good experience that God is preparing for you!

LESSON # 7: MAN'S REJECTION IS GOD'S PROTECTION

I am learning more each day that God truly *does* work out all things for our good. It took me some time to really accept God's sovereign hand in allowing that particular relationship to end. Before then, I would pray, "God, bring him back into my life!" Truthfully! But when God closes a door, know that it is because He sees so much further than what we can see. A friend of mine shared with me this powerful statement: "We cannot choose who our parents are. We cannot choose who our siblings are. We don't even have a choice in how our children will turn out. However, the only person that we do have a say so in, is our spouses." When I thought about it, I realized that when it comes to a spouse, you really need to make sure that it is God who is leading you to the right person. Can you imagine how different history would have been if Abraham had not married Sarah? What if Boaz had not married Ruth? I believe that right now, God is orchestrating the events for you to meet your spouse at the right place and the right time. The entire lineage of your children and your children's children is directly connected to whom you will ultimately marry. When you put it in that perspective, it is definitely wise to wait for the right person that God has already selected for you. Father knows best!

Although many of my close friends are already married, I know that God is preparing me during this season of waiting. Marriage is supposed to be for life. Therefore, regardless of how long it takes, when I finally meet the right man, it will be worth the wait. Please do not believe the lie of the enemy that something is "wrong with you" if you have ever been dumped. Just rest assured that God is omniscient and sometimes it is really a blessing in disguise when we don't get what we *think* we want. God may very well be sparing you from years of unnecessary heartache and turmoil. Just look at the children of Israel, when they *thought* they needed a king. Saul was a horrible leader and brought a great deal of misery to the children of Israel. Although he was tall, handsome, and "looked the part," he was not good for Israel. Likewise, you may be dating someone who is tall, handsome, and may appear to have a lot of things going for him, but God knows the heart of man. And what you think may be a good choice may be dead wrong.

Now I am very grateful that the relationship ended. God truly is sovereign; I believe that God may have just spared me from what I probably could not handle later down the road. He sees what we don't see!

LESSON # 8: BIRDS OF A FEATHER FARE MUCH BETTER

The whole theory of "opposites attracting," I've realized, needs to stay within the walls of a physics class. When it comes to developing a purposeful relationship with the member of the opposite sex that will lead to a God-honoring marriage, it needs to begin with a solid foundation based on similarities. I am in no way advocating that you marry someone who is exactly like you. A balanced relationship is one in which the man and the woman *complement* one another. Your gifts, natural abilities, and personality will need to complement your spouse's gifts, natural abilities and personality. However, when you find yourself in a relationship in which you have to completely revamp and change who you are as the individual that God created you to be to please another person, then there's a problem.

When the Lord brings two lives together to become one flesh, these two individuals will both bring to the table their own background experiences, values, morals, goals, and perspectives on life as the two build a life together. Marriage is a lifelong commitment. Therefore, evaluate your potential mate, and see what your similarities are in life.

Do you both have the same goals? What do you both enjoy doing? What are your passions, and do they line up together? Within a marriage, two people can either grow closer or grow apart through the years. When you are both old and gray and the beauty and charm have faded away, will you enjoy being around each other? These are some important questions to consider before you are married.

LESSON #9: THERE IS NOTHING WRONG WITH HIGH STANDARDS

This last lesson, I believe will really set someone's mind free. There was a time in my life (I no longer feel this way), when I would feel bad about having such high standards. I would often hear comments like, "Don't set your standards too high," or "You don't want to drive guys away." But honey, I have come to a place where I realize the worth and value that Christ has put on my life! Jesus Christ gave up His life for you and me, and what now makes us valuable is that the Father loves us. How amazing is that? When I finally grabbed a hold of this truth, I realized that I cannot throw around my time, affection, and love to just any Bozo off the street. I once read a quote that said: "You will only accept what you *believe* you deserve." Please do not make the mistake of settling for second best, for fear that no one better will come around. That is a lie of the enemy! You are a daughter of the King of Kings, which automatically makes you a princess. You deserve a prince, a son of the King. Stop settling for these paupers posing as princes! If you're still waiting on the Lord to bless you with a husband, just know that your *waiting time* is not *wasted time.*

There are a multitude of things you can do during this season: pursue higher education; take up a new hobby; sharpen the skills and gifts that God has graced you with to be a better servant in the kingdom; travel the world; learn how to cook—well; learn a new language; cultivate deeper relationships with friends and family or make new friends. So it may *appear* that there aren't many guys lined up to get your number. Rest assured that the right man, the one God has for you, will not be intimidated by a woman of God with a vision and purpose for her life. I believe that for myself, God is keeping me hidden long enough for my right man to find me. And when he does find you, ladies, he will truly say that you *are* his good thing!

I cannot stress this enough—don't lower your standards. Believe me; the right man will rise to the occasion to pursue you because he realizes that you truly are worth it.

LESSON # 10: LET GO OF ALL THE BAGGAGE

With this last lesson, let me encourage you ladies to not only allow the Lord to heal your heart from any past hurt, but also give over to Him any emotional baggage from previous relationships. Whether you've dated in the world before coming to know the Lord or have only dated guys in the kingdom, it is important that before the Lord allows you to embark in another relationship, you need to release all the "baggage." Don't make the next person have to pay for another person's mistake. Emotional baggage is not only limited to romantic relationships. Unresolved issues between you and your parents can also affect your future marital relationship. Perhaps you did not grow up with a father, or maybe you lacked an emotional bond with one or both parents. Take the time during your singlehood to evaluate your relationship with your parents. If there is any bitterness or unforgiveness still in your heart, take that to the Lord. You want to make sure, for the sake of your future spouse, that the Lord has dealt with any baggage you have. Bringing that into any relationship does not help either person in the relationship. Let it go!

Notes from

Lessons I've Learned about Dating

Confessions of a Bridesmaid

1. When the spiritual and the natural are in order in a man, it makes an irresistible total package! What are some of your expectations for a man before he pursues you?

2. How do you feel about an age gap? Are comfortable with a man courting you who is significantly *younger* or *older* than you?

3. How would you describe your relationship with the opposite sex? Do you have healthy friendships with both men and women?

4. How do you deal with rejection? We all will deal with hurt and pain from a broken relationship. Give God all the time He needs to heal your heart and deal with any underlying issues. In addition, talk about your feelings with a trusted friend. Pray it out. Cry it out. Be honest with the Lord about how you feel.

Confessions of a Bridesmaid

5. God is a God of relationship. It is important that we take into account how we treat the people that He has placed in our lives. This involves family, friends, coworkers, and neighbors. If you find yourself interested in a brother, first take an inventory of how he treats the people who are the closest in his life. How does he treat his mother and father? His sisters and brothers? What is like when he is around his friends? Is he a man of integrity on the job?

6. How would you describe *your* relationship with your family? How was your relationship with your father when you were growing up? Your mother? Ask the Lord to help you with these relationships first before you "leave and cleave" to a husband. Unresolved issues between you and your parents can resurface and affect your marital relationship in the future.

7. What qualities are you looking for in a future husband?

8. What are your expectations for marriage? Are they realistic?

9. What are some things *you* will bring into the relationship when you're married?

10. Describe the perfect first date.

Afterword

"And I heard, as it were, the voice of a great multitude, as the sound of many waters and as the sound of mighty thunderings, saying, 'Alleluia! For the Lord God Omnipotent reigns! Let us be glad and rejoice and give Him glory, for the marriage of the Lamb has come, and His wife has made herself ready. And to her it was granted to be arrayed in fine line, clean and bright, for the fine linen is the righteous acts of saints. Then he said to me, 'Write, "Blessed *are* those who are called to the marriage supper of the Lamb!"' And he said to me, 'These are the true sayings of God.'"[12]

Ladies, regardless of when you walk down the aisle, the Word of God declares that we are *already* a bride. That's right—we are the bride of Christ. Your relationship with Him is the most important relationship you could ever have. When we finally see the face of Jesus, there will be a wedding that takes place in heaven that cannot compare to the most extravagant wedding that could take place here on Earth. We will finally see Jesus, *our* Bridegroom. Our wedding dress will be a robe of white, representing a life that has been bought by the blood

---

12   Revelation 19:6–9 NKJV.

of Christ. You definitely need to make sure that you have an invitation to *this* wedding.

For those of you reading this today, who do not know the Lord, I invite you today to give your heart to Jesus Christ. It is simply a matter of realizing your need for a Savior, confessing your sins to the Lord, and turning away from those sins. Once you have made this confession of living a life for the Lord, congratulations! The Bible declares that you are now a child of God, a daughter of the King, and the bride of Christ. For those of you reading who are saved, I encourage you to grow in your love relationship with the Lord. He desires more of your heart, more of your worship, more of you; fall in love with Jesus again. If you are reading this today and may have turned away from the Lord for whatever the reason, I encourage you to come back to the Lord. He loves you, and His arms are open wide, waiting for you to return.

Encouraging Scriptures for the Single Woman

Delight yourself also in the LORD, and He shall give you the desires of your heart. (Psalm 37:4)

The LORD *is* good to those who wait for Him, to the soul *who* seeks Him. (Lamentations 3:25)

From the end of the earth I will cry to You, when my heart is overwhelmed; lead me to the rock that is higher than I. (Psalm 61:2)

I beseech you therefore, brethren, by the mercies of God, that you present your bodies a living sacrifice, holy, acceptable to God, *which is* your reasonable service.
(Romans 12:1)

Do not sorrow, for the joy of the LORD is your strength.
(Nehemiah 8:10)

He who *finds* a wife finds a good *thing,* and obtains favor from the LORD.
(Proverbs 18:22)

Keep your heart with all diligence, for out of it spring the issues of life.
(Proverbs 4:23)

Trust in the Lord with all your heart, and lean not on your own understanding; in all your ways acknowledge Him, And He shall direct your paths. (Proverbs 3:5)

Now to Him who is able to do exceedingly abundantly above all that we ask or think, according to the power that works in us.
(Ephesians 3:20)

For I know the plans I have for you, declares the LORD, plans to prosper you and not to harm you, plans to give you hope and a future.
(Jeremiah 29:11)

I praise you because I am fearfully and wonderfully made; your works are wonderful, I know that full well.
(Ps 139:4)

It is God's will that you should be sanctified: that you should avoid sexual immorality; that each of you should learn to control your own body in a way that is holy and honorable, not in passionate lust like the pagans, who do not know God; that in this matter no one should wrong or take advantage of a brother or sister. The Lord will punish all those

who commit such sins, as we told you and warned you before. For God did not call us to be impure, but to live a holy life.
(I Thessalonians 4:3-7)

Do not let your adornment be *merely* outward—arranging the hair, wearing gold, or putting on *fine* apparel— rather *let it be* the hidden person of the heart, with the incorruptible *beauty* of a gentle and quiet spirit, which is very precious in the sight of God. (1 Peter 3:3-4)

Who can find a virtuous wife? For her worth *is* far above rubies. (Proverbs 31:1)

Charm *is* deceitful and beauty *is* passing,
But a woman *who* fears the LORD, she shall be praised.
(Proverbs 31:30)

He who has begun a good work in you will complete *it* until the day of Jesus Christ. (Philippians 1:6)

Be anxious for nothing, but in everything by prayer and supplication, with thanksgiving, let your requests be made known to God;
(Philippians 4:6)

Finally, brethren, whatever things are true, whatever things *are* noble, whatever things *are* just, whatever things *are* pure, whatever things *are* lovely, whatever things *are* of good report, if *there is* any virtue and if *there is* anything praiseworthy—meditate on these things.
(Philippians 4:8)

For the LORD God *is* a sun and shield;

The LORD will give grace and glory;
No good *thing* will He withhold
from those who walk uprightly. (Psalm 84:11)

Now godliness with contentment is great gain.
(1 Timothy 6:6)

The steps of a *good* [woman] are ordered by the LORD,
And He delights in [her] way. (Psalm 37:23-24)

The LORD has appeared of old to me, saying: Yes, I have loved you with an everlasting love; Therefore with lovingkindness I have drawn you. (Jeremiah 31:3)

Or do you not know that your body is the temple of the Holy Spirit who is in you, whom you have from God, and you are not your own?
(1 Corinthians 6:9)

Be still before the Lord and wait patiently for him; (Ps 37:7)

"Blessed is the man who trusts in the LORD,
And whose hope is the LORD. (Jeremiah 17:7)

"For my thoughts are not your thoughts,
neither are your ways my ways," declares the LORD.
"As the heave ns are higher than the earth, so are my ways higher than your ways and my thoughts than your thoughts. (Isaiah 55: 8-9)

The LORD will perfect that which concerns me;
Your mercy, O LORD, endures forever;
Do not forsake the works of Your hands.
(Ps. 138:8)

The Lord your God is with you, he is mighty to save. He will take great delight in you, he will quiet you with his love, he will rejoice over you with singing." (Zephaniah 3:17)

For your Maker is your husband, The LORD of hosts is His name; and your Redeemer is the Holy One of Israel; He is called the God of the whole earth.
(Isaiah 54:5)

Flee from sexual immorality. All other sins a man commits are outside the body, but he who sins sexually sins against his own body. Do you not know that your body is a temple of the Holy Spirit, who is in you, whom you have received from God? You are not your own; you were bought with a price. Therefore, honor God with your body.
(1 Corinthians 6:18-20)

Flee also youthful lusts; but pursue righteousness, faith, love, peace with those who call on the Lord out of a pure heart.
(2 Timothy 2:22)

But those who wait on the LORD Shall renew *their* strength; They shall mount up with wings like eagles, They shall run and not be weary, They shall walk and not faint.
(Isaiah 40:31)

Those who sow in tears will reap with songs of joy. He who goes out weeping, carrying seed to sow, will return with songs of joy, carrying sheaves with him. (Ps 126: 5-6)

You number my wanderings; put my tears into Your bottle;
Are they not in your book? (Ps 56:8)

The LORD is your keeper; The LORD is your shade at your right hand. (Ps 121:5)

How lovely is your dwelling place, O Lord Almighty! My soul yearns, even faints, for the courts of the Lord; my heart and my flesh cry out for the living God. (Ps 84: 1-2)

Better is one day in your courts than a thousand elsewhere;
(Ps 84:10)

Many a man claims to have unfailing love, but a faithful man who can find? (Proverbs 20:6)

Imagine! His left hand cradling my head,
his right arm around my waist!
Oh, let me warn you, sisters in Jerusalem:
Don't excite love, don't stir it up,
until the time is ripe—and you're ready.
(Song of Solomon 8:4)

Make every effort to live in peace with everyone and to be holy; without holiness no one will see the Lord.
(Hebrews 12:14)

Let no one say when he is tempted, I am tempted by God; for God cannot be tempted by evil, nor does He Himself tempt anyone. But each one is tempted when he is drawn away by his own desires and enticed. Then, when desire has conceived, it gives birth to sin; and sin, when it is full-grown, brings forth death.
(James 1: 13-15)

Can two walk together, unless they are agreed?
(Amos 3:3)

I made a covenant with my eyes
not to look with lust at a young [man]. (Job 31:1)

Let the words of my mouth and the meditation of my heart
Be acceptable in Your sight, O LORD, my strength and my Redeemer.
(Psalm 19:14)

I will set before my eyes no vile thing. The deeds of faithless men I hate; they will not cling to me.
(Psalm 101:3)

Therefore, prepare your minds for action; be self-controlled; set your hope fully on the grace to be given you when Jesus Christ is revealed. As obedient children, do not conform to the evil desires you had when you lived in ignorance. But just as he who called you is holy, be holy in all you do; for it is written: Be holy, because I am holy.
(1 Peter 1:13-16)

Do not be yoked together with unbelievers. For what does righteousness and wickedness have in common? Or what fellowship can light have with darkness? What harmony is there between Christ and Belial? What does a believer have in common with an unbeliever? What agreement is there between the temple of God and idols? For we are the temple of the living God.
(2 Corinthians 6:14-16)

Since we have these promises, dear friends, let us purify ourselves from everything that contaminates body and spirit, perfecting holiness out of reverence for God. (2 Corinthians 7:1)

As the deer pants for the streams of water, so my soul pants for you, O God. (Psalm 42:1)

Create a pure heart, O God, and renew a steadfast spirit within me. (Psalm 51:10)

Where *there is* no counsel, the people fall; but in the multitude of counselors *there is* safety. (Proverbs 11:14)

Plans fail for lack of counsel, but with many advisers they succeed. (Proverbs 15:22)

Finally, brothers, whatever is true, whatever is noble, whatever is right, whatever is pure, whatever is lovely, whatever is admirable—if anything is excellent or praiseworthy—think about such things. (Philippians 4:8)

Love the Lord your God with all your heart and with all your soul and with all your strength. (Deuteronomy 6:5)

Do not let this Book of the Law depart from your mouth; meditate on it day and night, so that you may be careful to do everything written in it.
(Joshua 1:8)

For you know that it was not with perishable things such as silver or gold that you were redeemed from the empty way of life handed down to you from your forefathers, but with the precious blood of Christ, a lamb without blemish or defect. (1 Peter 1: 18-19)

But you are a chosen people, a royal priesthood, a holy nation, a people belonging to God, that you may declare the praises of him who called you out of darkness into his wonderful light.
(1 Peter 1: 9)

Dear friends, I urge you, as aliens and strangers in the world, to abstain from sinful desires, which war against your soul.
(1 Peter 1: 11)

Each one should use whatever gift he has received to serve others, faithfully administering God's grace in its various forms. If anyone speaks, he should do it as one speaking the very words of God. If anyone serves, he should do it with the strength God provides, so that in all things God may be praised through Jesus Chris. To him be the glory and the power for ever and ever. Amen.
(1 Peter 4: 10-11)

Be self-controlled and alert. Your enemy the devil prowls around like a roaring lion looking for someone to devour. (1 Peter 5:8)

As a prisoner for the Lord, then, I urge you to live a life worthy of the calling you have received. Be completely humble and gentle, be patient, bearing with one another in love.
(Ephesians 4: 1-2)

Teach us to number our days aright, that we may gain a heart of wisdom. (Psalm 90:12)

Satisfy us in the morning with your unfailing love, that we may sing for joy and be glad all our days. (Psalm 90:14)

May the favor of the Lord our God rest upon us; establish the work of our hands for us—yes, establish the work of our hands.
(Psalm 90:17)

For as high as the heavens are above the earth so great is his love for those who fear him; as far as the east is from the west, so far has he removed our transgressions from us. (Psalm 102: 11-12).

Who is a God like you, who pardons sin and forgives the transgression of the remnant of his inheritance? You do not stay angry forever but delight to show mercy. You will again have compassion on us; you will tread our sins underfoot and hurl all our iniquities into the depths of the sea.
(Micah 7:18-19)

Love is patient, love is kind. It does not envy, it does not boast, it is not proud. It is not rude, it is not self-seeking, it is not easily angered, it keeps no record of wrongs. Love does not delight in evil but rejoices with the truth. It always protects, always trusts, always hopes, always perseveres. Love never fails.
(1 Corinthians 13: 4-8)

And now these three remain: faith, hope and love. But the greatest of these is love. (1 Corinthians 13:13)

And so we know and rely on the love God has for us. God is love. Whoever lives in love lives in God, and God in him…We love because he first loved us. (1 John 4:16,19)

About the Author

Larissa Dayana Jean is a young woman making the most of her single years by making a great impact in the Kingdom of God and her community. Born in Port au Prince, Haiti, Larissa and her family relocated to the United States when she was almost two years of age. She spent her childhood in Boston, Massachusetts, and with the influence of her mother, became an avid reader and writer.

On July 17, 1997, the Lord allowed Larissa and her immediate family to relocate again, this time to Georgia. While under the leadership of her first pastor, Reverend Brave Laverdure, Senior Pastor of the Good Samaritan Haitian Alliance Church, the Lord knocked on the door to her heart. On April 4, 1999, Easter Sunday, Larissa began her relationship with the Lord Jesus Christ. From that point, she became very active within her youth ministry and had an opportunity to serve as a mentor and teacher in a ministry for young girls entitled, Girls Living Out Righteousness In Action, also known as GLORIA.

After graduating from Berkmar High School, Larissa enrolled at the University of Georgia, where she later graduated with a dual degree in Spanish and Foreign Language Education. During her time as a UGA student, the Lord opened even more doors for her to minister to young women. As a Resident Assistant on the University of Georgia's campus, she had the opportunity to pour into the lives of sixty young collegiate women in a span of two years. In addition to the young women in the dormitories, she had the honor to serve two years as the campus ministry president for Joshua Generation Campus Ministry, as well two years for Omega Campus Ministry. It was during this time that the Lord began to mold her as a teacher of the word of God. Then, in 2005, the Lord led Larissa to Omega Worship Center, under the leadership of her pastors, Dr. Yulonda Z. Lewis and Bishop Rayfield Lewis. Through her spiritual growth in this ministry, the Lord began tugging on her heart and slowly showing her role in the lives of young single women in the Kingdom.

Larissa's passion is to serve both youth and young women. She loves being able to pour into the life of another sister and help her realize that her identity is truly found in Christ Jesus. When Larissa began to really seek the Lord about His purpose for her life as it pertained to young women in the body of Christ, He reminded her of a dream that He put in her heart as a little girl—writing books. The scripture that God pressed upon her heart during that time of seeking Him was "Write the vision and make it plain on tablets that he may run who reads it"(Habakkuk 2:2). At that point, Larissa realized that the Lord wanted to use her to help other young women through her own story. Therefore, in October of 2009, she began writing her first book, *Lessons Learned as a Bridesmaid*.

Through her book, her desire is to see young women in the Kingdom know their true identity in Christ and fall in love with the Father. She wants young women to understand that their identity is not wrapped up in their marital status. Her prayer is that single women will use their waiting time to serve the Lord with *passion*. She encourages all single women to wait *patiently* on the Lord until He sends them a godly husband. Larissa is now a Spanish teacher and lives in Lawrenceville, Georgia.